THE OFFICIAL
COLCHESTER UNITED
QUIZ BOOK

THE OFFICIAL COLCHESTER UNITED QUIZ BOOK

COMPILED BY
CHRIS COWLIN

APEX PUBLISHING LTD

First published in 2006 by
Apex Publishing Ltd
PO Box 7086, Clacton on Sea, Essex, CO15 5WN, England

www.apexpublishing.co.uk

British Library Cataloguing-in-Publication Data
A catalogue record for this book
is available from the British Library

ISBN 1-904444-88-1

Typeset in 10.5pt Chianti BdIt Win95BT

Cover Design: Andrew Macey

Printed and bound in Great Britain

Author's Note:
Please can you contact me: ChrisCowlin@btconnect.com if you find any mistakes/errors in this book as I would like to put them right on any future reprints of this book. I would also like to hear from Colchester United fans who have enjoyed the test!

This book is an official product of Colchester United Football Club

*I would like to dedicate this book to my son Harry
and also to Phil Parkinson and every player in the
promotion winning squad during the 2005/2006 season.*

FOREWORD

I must say it was a privilege to be asked to provide the foreword for this official Colchester United quiz book and it is a pleasure to accept. As a player, I have endured many a long journey across the country going to our away games, so any good form of entertainment is a must. Believe me, the competitive nature of all the footballers that I have ever known will ensure that many an argument will erupt about who is the cleverest on the coach. I hope I have a bit of an advantage, having been at the club longer than all the others.

I have been at the club for a good few years now and there have been many ups and downs in my time here at Layer Road. I have worked under a few managers since I broke into the first team whilst still a youth player in December 1995, including getting promoted with both Steve Wignall and Phil Parkinson at the helm. I have played alongside too many players to remember them all, but it was great to learn my trade as a youngster with the likes of Mark Kinsella and Jason Dozzell at the club.

That first game for me came at Hereford on a freezing cold December Saturday and I remember we left Layer Road at about half past seven in the morning. I was named as a substitute for the match with Tony Dennis and David Gregory and it was a real struggle to keep our feet from going numb from the cold. I went on in the second half to make my debut and I'm sure my feet only warmed up just before the referee blew the final whistle. We got a 1-1 draw thanks to a Simon Betts goal and I was a very happy young man making the journey back home that night.

Over the years, there have been some very memorable times

for me at Colchester United and I have made lots of friends, both on and off the pitch, in my career here in North Essex. The two promotions that I was involved in were obviously great experiences and the support I had during my Testimonial year was tremendous. The encouragement I had from U's supporters near and far when I was injured will be forever remembered and they were a massive help during those long months back in 2004/05.

Obviously, that serious knee injury was the biggest low point of my time at the club and I must admit there were a few occasions where it crossed my mind that I might have played my last game of football. The backing I had from all the staff at the club was excellent and I am grateful that the club stuck by me when I was out of action for so long. I had suffered other injuries before that but I was never out for long so I was very frustrated to be injured for the whole season.

When I missed the deciding penalty in the Wembley final in 1997 against Carlisle, I thought I had reached as low as any footballer could feel. That knee injury however, put things into perspective and certainly eclipsed the disappointment I felt after that miss. I have enjoyed every second of my football since I have been fit again and wouldn't wish a serious injury on my worst enemy.

Those two promotions that I mentioned earlier have given me great memories to treasure and the best thing is they were achieved in totally different ways. We were so disappointed after our last league match of the season in 1997/8 when we just missed out on automatic promotion. But, we bounced back from that disappointment to win promotion to League One, as it is now, with the victory at Wembley. I came on as a substitute in the second half and the win more than made up for the penalty miss the previous year.

In the successful 2005/6, we managed to gain automatic

promotion and went up to the Championship as League One Runners-Up. Being captain was a great honour and once again, a promotion made up for the massive low I had the previous season, this time it had been my injury. Those promotions will of course go down in Colchester United history but will also provide hours of discussion amongst players and supporters alike.

All U's fans will know that Championship football was secured on that day in May 2006 but this quiz book provides plenty of questions about our promotion season that could catch out even the staunchest of U's fans. The football club was obviously here a long time before I arrived and I was amazed at the number of facts I have uncovered about the place whilst going through the various sections of the book.

Every book that is sold also generates much-needed funds for the Colchester United Community Sports Trust and this could help the club unearth another John White or Greg Halford. The work the Trust does in and around Colchester is a credit to the club and hopefully, these monies will help it continue to bring sport to all children in the area. I hope you enjoy the book as much as I have and I am sure it will provoke discussion and argument in equal measure before the answers are revealed.

Karl Duguid

INTRODUCTION

I would first of all like to thank Karl Duguid for writing the foreword to this book, I am very grateful for his help on this project and I am sure every fan with agree with me in saying he has been a truly passionate player for the U's during his playing career.

I would also like to thank the following people for their comments and support for this book: Mark Kinsella, Tony Adcock, Bobby Hunt, Micky Cook, Phil Parkinson, Jim Smith, Lomana Tresor Lua Lua, Roger Osborne and Marie Partner.

I would personally like to thank Colchester United legend David Gregory for all his help on this book and securing the foreword from Karl and the various endorsements on the back cover, he has been a great help to me on this project, which I am extremely grateful for.

I am honoured to donate £1 from each book sale to 'The Colchester United Community Sports Trust'. For more details on the trust please look at the back of this book.

I hope you enjoy this book, it was a pleasure compiling it as I learnt so much about the club and the past players - I hope it brings back some fond memories of the U's wins and the various matches at Layer Road.

In closing, I would like to thank all my friends and family for encouraging me to complete this book.

Chris Cowlin

Chris Cowlin

2005/2006 -
UP TO THE CHAMPIONSHIP

1.   Which manager guided the U's to promotion?

2.   Who did Colchester play on the opening day of the season - Gillingham, Hartlepool United or Walsall?

3.   Against which club did Colchester play their final League One game and get promotion to the Championship?

4.   Which player did the U's have on loan from Tottenham Hotspur during the season - Johnnie Jackson, Ledley King or Mark Yeates?

5.   Which player wore the number 12 shirt?

6.   Which Premiership side did Colchester play in the 5th round of the FA Cup, losing 3-1 - Manchester United, Birmingham City or Chelsea?

7.   During August 2005 Colchester won one game, against which club?

8.   How many League goals did Greg Halford score during the season - 5, 6 or 7?

9.   Colchester played 46 League games. How many did they win?

10. How many League goals did Chris Iwelumo score for the U's - 15, 17 or 19?

CLUB HISTORY & STADIUM

11. In what year was Colchester United Football Club formed - 1927, 1937 or 1947?

12. Which team did Colchester beat 4-3 at Layer Road in August 2006 for it to be their first League win of the season?

13. Colchester's record home attendance is 19,072. Who did they play against in the FA Cup in November 1948 - Leeds United, Manchester United or Reading?

14. Who was appointed Colchester manager in July 2006?

15. In which season did Colchester United first play in the Football League - 1948/1949, 1949/1950 or 1950/1951?

16. Colchester's record signing is £50,000. Which two players did they buy in 1998 and then in 2001 costing that amount?

17. Which team beat Colchester United 8-0 in October 1988, making the score Colchester's biggest ever defeat - Leyton Orient, Barnet or Northampton Town?

18. Which player has made the most appearances for the club with 631, between 1969 and 1984?

19. What is the name of the Cup that Colchester United won during 1970/1971 - Watney Cup, League Cup or FA Cup?

20. Which player scored a record 37 goals in the 1961/1962 season?

NATIONALTIES

PLEASE MATCH THE PLAYER WITH THEIR NATIONALITY

21.	Karl Duguid	*Irish*
22.	Gareth Williams	*Irish*
23.	Mark Kinsella	Democratic Republic of Congo
24.	George Elokobi	*English*
25.	Chris Iwelumo	*Scottish*
26.	Mark Yeates	*Welsh*
27.	Richard Garcia	*English*
28.	Lomana Tresor Lua-Lua	*Australian*
29.	Pat Baldwin	*Cameroon*
30.	Marino Keith	*Scottish*

POT LUCK - 1

31. From which club did Colchester sign Geraint Williams from during July 1998 on a free transfer?

32. Where in Essex was Liam Chilvers born - Colchester, Clacton on Sea or Chelmsford?

33. For which London club did Wayne Brown play while on loan in 2001?

34. Can you name the goalkeeper that Colchester signed in July 2004 on a free transfer from Grimsby Town - Andy Walker, Simon Brown or Aidan Davison?

35. During the 2002/2003 season, how many League goals did Kemal Izzet score for the U's?

36. Which former England manager signed Lomana Tresor Lua-Lua for Newcastle United in 2000 from the U's - Graham Taylor, Bobby Robson or Glenn Hoddle?

37. In what year did Mick Wadsworth take over as U's manager?

38. Scott McGleish spent 3 months on loan at Layer Road during 1996, making 15 League appearances. How many goals did he score - 4, 5 or 6?

39. When the U's signed Stephen Hunt on a free transfer in 2004, from which club did they sign him?

40. For which Premiership team did Neil Danns play during the 2002/2003 season - Bolton Wanderers, Blackburn Rovers or Manchester City?

WHERE DID THEY GO?

PLEASE MATCH THE PLAYER WITH THE CLUB
HE JOINED WHEN HE LEFT THE U'S

41.	Simon Brown	Charlton Athletic
42.	Mick Stockwell	Kettering Town
43.	Rowan Vine	Southend United
44.	Paul Abrahams	Boston United
45.	Scott McGleish	Hibernian
46.	Jamie Cade	Gravesend & Northfleet
47.	Mark Kinsella	Portsmouth
48.	Roy McDonough	Northampton Town
49.	Bobby Bowry	Heybridge Swifts
50.	Gavin Johnson	Crawley Town

STEVE WHITTON

51.   In what year was Steve born - 1958, 1959 or 1960?

52.   How much did Colchester pay for Steve?

53.   Where did Colchester sign Steve from - Norwich City, Southend United or Ipswich Town?

54.   Against which team did Steve score his first goals in a 3-1 win in April 1994?

55.   Which Midlands side did Colchester beat 3-2 at home during September 1994 when Steve scored one and Mark Kinsella two - Walsall, Aston Villa or Birmingham City?

56.   In what year did Steve arrive at Layer Road?

57.   In which year did Steve take over as manager of the U's - 1997, 1998 or 1999?

58.   Against which team did Steve score his only goal of the 1997/1998 season during January 1998 in a 1-1 away draw?

59.   Who replaced Steve as U's manager in 2003 - Mike Walker, Steve Wignall or Phil Parkinson?

60.   For which team did Steve play between 1983 and 1986?

NAME THE YEAR - 1

MATCH THE EVENT WITH THE YEAR IN WHICH IT TOOK PLACE

61.	Tony Adcock signed from Luton Town on a free transfer	1961
62.	Colchester beat Leamington 9-1 in the FA Cup (1st round)	1992
63.	Leyton Orient beat Colchester 8-0 in Division 4	1971
64.	Carl Emberson signed from Millwall costing £25,000	1995
65.	Colchester finished 2nd in League One behind Southend United	2005
66.	Colchester beat Leeds United 3-2 in the FA Cup 5th round	2006
67.	Mark Kinsella left Colchester to join Charlton Athletic	1989
68.	Colchester beat Bradford City 9-1 in Division 4	1994
69.	Colchester lost 3-1 to Chelsea in the 5th round of the FA Cup	1996
70.	Steve McGavin played his first game for the U's	2006

LOMANA TRESOR LUA-LUA

71. Which Colchester manager gave Lomana his U's debut - Phil Parkinson, Steve Wignall or Mick Wadsworth?

72. Who did Lomana score against on his U's debut during 1998/1999?

73. When Lomana left Layer Road, which Premier League club did he sign for - Manchester City, Portsmouth or Newcastle United?

74. Which Premier League team did Lomana go on loan to during January 2004 and later sign a permanent deal with them?

75. In what year was Lomana born - 1978, 1980 or 1982?

76. Which country does Lomana represent at international level?

77. Against which London club did Lomana score a League Cup hat-trick in August 2000 - Fulham, Queens Park Rangers or Barnet?

78. Lomana scored two goals in a 3-1 home win against Bournemouth in January 2000. Who scored the other?

79. Against which team was Lomana's last U's goal - Tranmere Rovers, Oldham Athletic or Queens Park Rangers?

80. Lomana scored in the nine-goal thriller, the 5-4 home win against Bristol Rovers in January 2000. Which two players both scored two apiece for the U's?

PHIL PARKINSON

81.   Phil took over from Steve Whitton as manager of
        Colchester, in what year - 2002, 2003 or 2004?

82.   For which team did Phil play between 1988 and 1992?

83.   In what year was Phil born - 1966, 1967 or 1968?

84.   Which club did Phil sign for as an apprentice in 1985 and
        later leave in 1988?

85.   In 2002 Phil was awarded his testimonial game. Who
        was it against - Scotland XI, England XI or Republic of
        Ireland XI?

86.   What is Phil's nickname at Layer Road?

87.   Phil was 'player of the year' for his club in two
        consecutive years. Which years - 1994 and 1995, 1996
        and 1997, or 1998 and 1999?

88.   In which position did Phil play during his playing career?

89.   For which club did Phil play between 1992 and 2003 -
        Reading, Sheffield United or Sheffield Wednesday?

90.   Following on from the previous question, Phil played
        426 games for the club, scoring how many goals?

COLCHESTER MANAGERS

MATCH THE MANAGER WITH HIS PERIOD
IN CHARGE OF THE CLUB

91.	Steve Whitton	1994
92.	Mike Walker	1982 to 1983
93.	Roy McDonough	1990
94.	Allan Hunter	1972 to 1975
95.	George Burley	1995 to 1999
96.	Jim Smith	1999 to 2003
97.	Ted Fenton	1991 to 1994
98.	Steve Wignall	1968 to 1972
99.	Dick Graham	1946 to 1948
100.	Mick Mills	1986 to 1987

JASON DOZZELL

101. In what year did Jason join Colchester United - 1997, 1998 or 1999?

102. In what position did Jason play for the U's?

103. For which club did Jason play between 1984 and 1993 - Norwich City, Southend United or Ipswich Town?

104. How many goals did Jason score in his first season at Layer Road?

105. Jason scored his first Colchester goal in October 1998, against which club - Macclesfield Town, Blackpool or Manchester City?

106. How many League goals did Jason score during his Colchester career?

107. Which manager gave Jason his Colchester debut - Mick Wadsworth, Steve Wignall or Phil Parkinson?

108. In October 1999 Jason scored a brace in a 5-2 away defeat to which club?

109. On the opening day of the 1998/1999 season, Jason scored the only, winning goal against which club - Oldham Athletic, Southend United or Chesterfield?

110. Which London club did Jason sign for in 1993 from Ipswich Town?

KARL DUGUID

111. Against which team did Karl make his U's League debut in December 1995 in a 1-1 draw?

112. Karl scored one League goal during his first season at Layer Road, against whom - Northampton Town, Luton Town or Torquay United?

113. Which manager gave Karl his debut at Layer Road?

114. Karl scored in a 3-1 home win against Wigan Athletic in October 1996, but which two players scored the other goals - Tony Adcock and David Gregory, David Gregory and Neil Gregory, or Tony Adcock and Steve Whitton?

115. In how many League games did Karl play during the 2005/2006 promotion success?

116. Karl missed out on the whole of the 2004/2005 season through injury, but what was the injury - broken arm, torn knee ligament or broken foot?

117. In December 2005 Colchester beat which team 2-1 at the National Hockey Stadium, with Karl scoring?

118. What is Karl's nickname at Colchester - Karlo, Doogie or Dodgy?

119. Karl scored in a 2-1 home win against which team in December 2003?

120. During 2005/2006 which squad number did Karl wear - 7, 8 or 9?

HAT-TRICK HEROES - 1

*MATCH THE PLAYER WITH THE GAME IN WHICH
HE SCORED A HAT-TRICK FOR THE U'S*

121.   v. Queens Park Rangers (A)
       August 2000, Won 4-1   Tom English

122.   v. Torquay United (H)
       September 1995, Won 5-2   Mike Masters

123.   v. Bury (H)
       September 1993, Won 4-1   Simon Lowe

124.   v. Barrow (H)
       May 1992, Won 5-0   Tony English

125.   v. Slough Town (A)
       August 1991, Won 4-2   Tony Adcock

126.   v. Bath City (H)
       August 1991, Won 5-0   L. T. Lua-Lua

127.   v. Stockport County (H)
       March 1987, Won 5-1   Gary Bennett

128.   v. Torquay United (H)
       September 1986, Won 3-0   Roy McDonough

129.   v. Peterborough United (H)
       April 1986, Won 5-0   Steve Brown

130.   v. Preston North End (H)
       April 1986, Won 4-0   Tony English

GEORGE BURLEY

131. In which year did George arrive as manager of the U's - 1994, 1995 or 1996?

132. Who did George replace as U's manager?

133. Against which club was George's first game in charge - Gillingham, Exeter City or Torquay United?

134. How old was George Burley when he took charge at Layer Road?

135. George was appointed manager after a spell as player/manager at which Scottish club - Hibernian, Greenock Morton or Motherwell?

136. Who did George appoint as his assistant manager at Colchester?

137. In how many League games did George play for the U's during 1994/1995 - 6, 7 or 8?

138. Which club did George leave for to join as manager?

139. Against which side did George record his first League win for the U's in a 1-0 win - Scarborough, Luton Town or Barnsley?

140. Of which team was George appointed manager in December 2005?

BOBBY HUNT

141. In what year was Bobby born in Colchester - 1940, 1942 or 1944?

142. Bobby played 149 games for the U's, but how many goals did he score?

143. In which position did Bobby play - centre back, centre midfield or centre forward?

144. Which U's manager handed Bobby his debut at Layer Road?

145. Bobby Hunt currently holds the record at Colchester United for scoring the highest number of goals in a season, achieved during 1961/1962 in Division 4. How many goals - 37, 39 or 41?

146. For which London club did Bobby play between 1966 and 1967?

147. Bobby scored 4 goals in the same game in December 1961, against which team in Division 4 - Blackpool, Bournemouth or Bradford City?

148. Bobby scored 4 goals in another game in the same season in April 1962, against which team again in Division 4?

149. Bobby signed from Ipswich Town to which team in 1970 and later left in 1973 - West Ham United, Charlton Athletic or Chelsea?

150. When Bobby left Colchester in 1964, which club did he sign for?

MARK KINSELLA

151. What nationality is Mark - Scottish, English or Irish?

152. How many international caps did Mark win for his country, scoring three goals?

153. In what season did Mark make his U's debut - 1988/1989, 1989/1990 or 1990/1991?

154. Against which Division 4 team did Mark make his debut in a 2-2 draw as a substitute?

155. For which Midlands team did Mark play between 2002 and 2004 - Aston Villa, West Bromwich Albion or Walsall?

156. Which U's manager gave Mark his debut at Layer Road?

157. Against which country did Mark make his full international debut - Germany, England or Czech Republic?

158. During 1994/1995 Mark played in all 42 League games for the U's, scoring how many goals - 6, 8 or 10?

159. On New Year's Day 1996 Mark scored after 15 seconds against which side in a 3-2 away win - Walsall, Wimbledon or Torquay United?

160. When Mark left Colchester in 1996, which top-flight team did he join?

1971 FA CUP RUN

161. In the 5th round Colchester beat which top-flight club 3-2 at Layer Road - Liverpool, Tottenham Hotspur or Leeds United?

162. Following on from the previous question, which two players scored the three goals for the U's?

163. Who knocked Colchester out of the FA Cup in the quarter final - West Bromwich Albion, Coventry City or Everton?

164. In the 4th round (replay) the U's beat Rochdale, by what scoreline?

165. Who was the U's manager during this FA Cup run - Dick Graham, Allan Hunter or Denis Mocham?

166. Which goalkeeper played in all seven FA Cup matches?

167. Colchester's Ray Crawford scored a first-round hat-trick against which club - Rotherham, Ringmer or Southend United?

168. What record did Colchester create when they made it to the quarter-finals?

169. What was the attendance at home to Leeds United in the 3-2 home win - 14,000, 15,000 or 16,000?

170. Which team did Colchester beat 3-0 at home in the 2nd round?

MICK STOCKWELL

171. Where was Mick born - Chelmsford, Chester or Ipswich?

172. Which team did Mick sign from to join the U's?

173. Which U's manager signed Mick for Colchester United in 2000 - Mick Wadsworth, Steve Whitton or Phil Parkinson?

174. How much did Colchester pay for Mick?

175. Mick made his debut in August 2000, against which club away from home with a 0-0 score - Sunderland, Southend United or Swindon Town?

176. Mick scored his first U's goal in September 2000 in a 3-1 home win, against which side?

177. In November 2001 Mick scored two goals for the U's against Wigan Athletic in a 3-2 away win. Who got the other U's goal - Ross Johnson, Scott McGleish or David Gregory?

178. Mick played his last game for Colchester in May 2003 in a 1-0 home defeat to which London side?

179. How many goals (in all competitions) did Mick score for Colchester United in his first season at the club - 9, 11 or 13?

180. In July 2003 Mick left Layer Road and signed for which side on a free transfer?

BIG COLCHESTER WINS - 1

MATCH THE GAME WITH COLCHESTER'S WINNING SCORE

181. *v. Chesterfield (A)*
August 2001, Division 2   Won 7-1

182. *v. Bristol Rovers (H)*
January 2000, Division 2   Won 5-2

183. *v. Macclesfield Town (H)*
March 1998, Division 3   Won 4-0

184. *v. Lincoln City (H)*
November 1996, Division 3   Won 6-3

185. *v. Torquay United (H)*
September 1995, Associate Members Cup   Won 5-0

186. *v. Yeading (H)*
November 1994, FA Cup   Won 5-1

187. *v. Fulham (H)*
April 1995, Division 3   Won 5-4

188. *v. Wycombe Wanderers (A)*
September 1993, Division 3   Won 7-1

189. *v. Bath City (H)*
August 1991, Vauxhall Conference   Won 5-2

190. *v. Yeovil Town (H)*
September 1991, Vauxhall Conference   Won 5-2

DAVID GREGORY

191. Which club did David sign from to join the U's in 1995 - Ipswich Town, Peterborough United or Cambridge United?

192. Against which club did David score two goals in the play off semi-final, second leg in May 1998 in a 3-1 home win?

193. David scored the only goal in the Division 3 play-off final in May 1998, against which team - Barnet, Torquay United or Doncaster Rovers?

194. For which East Anglian side did David play between 1987 and 1995, making 32 League appearances and scoring two goals?

195. At which Essex side did David finish his playing career in 2004 - Canvey Island, Clacton Town or Colchester United?

196. During 1996/1997 David scored one goal, against which club?

197. How many League goals did David score during his spell at Colchester United - 17, 19 or 21?

198. Where in England was David born in 1970?

199. Against which side did David make his U's debut in January 1996 in a 3-2 home win - Barnet, Hull City or Brentford?

200. Which manager brought David to Layer Road?

WHERE DID THEY COME FROM?

201.	Thomas Pinault	Chelsea
202.	Gavin Johnson	Plymouth Argyle
203.	Chris Fry	Cannes
204.	Sam Stockley	Arsenal
205.	Pat Baldwin	Middlesbrough
206.	Mark Warren	Dunfermline
207.	Andy Myers	Hereford
208.	Jamie Cade	Notts County
209.	Liam Chilvers	Bradford City
210.	Marino Keith	Oxford United

TONY ADCOCK

211. Where was Tony born - London, Colchester or Birmingham?

212. In what position did Tony play for the U's?

213. When Tony signed for the U's for his second spell in 1995, which club did he sign from - Peterborough United, Bradford City or Luton Town?

214. Against which club did Tony make his U's debut in May 1981 as an 18-year-old?

215. Which manager gave Tony his U's debut in 1981 - Bobby Roberts, Jim Smith or Allan Hunter?

216. Against which club did Tony score his first goals in September 1981?

217. Against which club did Tony score his first U's hat-trick in January 1983 in a 4-3 home win - Blackpool, Crewe Alexandra or Derby County?

218 Tony scored an Auto Windscreen Shield hat-trick in a 5-2 home win in September 1995, against which club?

219. How many goals did Tony score during 1983/1984 in all competitions for the U's - 31, 33 or 35?

220. During 1984/1985 Tony scored two League hat-tricks, against which clubs?

STEVE McGAVIN

221. In which year was Steve born - 1967, 1969 or 1971?

222. When Steve re-signed for Colchester for his second spell at the club in 1999, where did he sign from?

223. For which Essex team did Steve play during 1999, making 11 League appearances - Canvey Island, Clacton Town or Southend United?

224. Against which Vauxhall Conference side did Steve make his U's League debut in a 2-1 away win in April 1991?

225. Which manager gave Steve his debut in 1991 - Micks Mills, George Burley or Ian Atkins?

226. Against which team did Steve score his first U's goals in August 1991 in a 5-0 win?

227. Steve scored in a 4-1 home win against Bury in Division 3 in September 1993. Which player scored a hat-trick in the game - Steve Whitton, Steve Brown or Mark Kinsella?

228. Which manager brought Steve back to Layer Road for a second spell in 1999?

229. In what position did Steve play for the U's - goalkeeper, midfield or forward?

230. For which Midlands team did Steve play between 1994 and 1995?

NAME THE YEAR - 2

231. Simon Clark signed from Leyton
     Orient on a free transfer   1992

232. Mick Wadsworth arrived
     and left as manager   1972

233. Colchester record their record
     attendance in the FA Cup against Reading   1987

234. Peter Crawley signed for the U's
     from Barnet on a free transfer   1999

235. Jim Smith takes the job at Layer
     Road as player/manager   2000

236. Alec Chamberlain signs for the
     U's from Ipswich Town   1986

237. Mike Walker was appointed
     U's manager   1986

238. Tony Adcock left and signed
     for Manchester City for £75,000   1999

239. Richard Wilkins signs for
     Colchester from Haverhill Rovers   1948

240. Steve Wignall leaves
     as Colchester manager   1982

MICKY COOK

241. Micky made his U's debut in October 1969, against which club - Wrexham, Swansea City or Bristol City?

242. On New Year's Day 1972 Micky scored his first U's goal, against which Division 4 side?

243. Which manger handed Micky his U's debut - Nell Franklin, Denis Mocham or Dick Graham?

244. In what position did Micky play for Colchester?

245. April 1976 saw Micky's testimonial match at Layer Road, against which team in a 2-1 U's win - Norwich City, Southend United or Ipswich Town?

246. Which manager was in charge when Micky played his last game for Colchester?

247. In which season did Micky win 'player of the year' - 1969/1970, 1971/1972 or 1973/1974?

248. During February 1983 Micky scored his only goal of the season in a 1-0 win against which side?

249. Micky played in every League game during 1978/1979. Which other U's player did the same - Mike Walker, Steve Foley or Trevor Lee?

250. Micky made a record number of appearances for the U's - how many?

HAT-TRICK HEROES - 2

MATCH THE PLAYER WITH THE GAME IN
WHICH HE SCORED A HAT-TRICK

251. v. Southend United (H)
      January 1986, Won 4-1   Colin Garwood

252. v. Southend United (A)
      October 1985, Won 4-2   Tony Adcock

253. v. Cambridge United (H)
      September 1985, Won 4-1   Ian Allinson

254. v. Chesterfield (H)
      February 1985, Won 3-1   Perry Groves

255. v. Southend United (H)
      August 1984, Drew 3-3   Bobby Gough

256. v. Wealdstone (H)
      December 1983, Won 4-0   Tony Adcock

257. v. Crewe Alexandra (H)
      January 1983, Won 4-3   Perry Groves

258. Mansfield Town (A)
      November 1981, Won 3-1   Tony Adcock

259. Oxford United (H)
      November 1978, Won 4-2   Keith Bowen

260. Bournemouth (Vicarage Road)
      December 1977, Won 4-1   Tony Adcock

WAYNE BROWN

261. From which team did Colchester sign Wayne in 2004 - Ipswich Town, Queens Park Rangers or Watford?

262. Against which team did Wayne score a vital goal for the U's' push for promotion to the Championship in April 2006 in a 1-0 home win?

263. Wayne made his U's debut against which team - Shrewsbury Town, Sheffield United or Coventry City?

264. Against which Welsh team did Wayne score his only goal of the season during 2004/2005?

265. For which team did Wayne make two appearances during 1997 whilst on loan - Colchester United, Chester City or Charlton Athletic?

266. Which team did Colchester beat 9-1 in the FA Cup 1st round in November 2005, with Wayne scoring one of the goals?

267. Wayne scored in November 2005 in a 5-0 home win at Gillingham. Which two U's players scored two apiece - Greg Halford and Jamie Cureton, Greg Halford and Chris Iwelumo, or Kevin Watson and Pat Baldwin?

268. For which team did Wayne play between 1995 and 2002?

269. In which season did Wayne win 'player of the year' - 2003/2004, 2004/2005 or 2005/2006?

270. Which manager signed Wayne for the U's?

JOE DUNNE

271. What nationality is Joe - Irish, Welsh or English?

272. From which club did Colchester sign Joe in 1996?

273. How many League goals did Joe score during his Colchester United career (both spells at the club) - 4, 5 or 6?

274. Against which club did Joe make his debut in March 1996 in a 2-1 defeat?

275. Joe opened the scoring in the 6-3 away win in August 2001 against which team - Chester City, Chesterfield or Derby County?

276. In January 2001 Joe scored for the U's away against Oxford United. What was the score?

277. In Joe's first season at Layer Road he scored one League goal, against which side in April 1996 - Mansfield Town, Rochdale or Bury?

278. Joe left Layer Road for which side in August 1999 only to return to Colchester in December 1999?

279. Following on from the previous question, which manager re-signed Joe for the U's - Mick Wadsworth, Phil Parkinson or Steve Whitton?

280. Against which team did Joe score the winning goal in a 1-0 away win in March 1998 in Division 3?

BIG COLCHESTER WINS - 2

MATCH THE GAME WITH COLCHESTER'S WINNING SCORE

281. **Kettering Town (H)**
     October 1991, Bob Lord Trophy   5-2

282. **Burton Albion (H)**
     November 1991, FA Cup   4-0

283. **Barrow (H)**
     May 1992, Vauxhall Conference   4-1

284. **Northwich Victoria (H)**
     September 1990, Vauxhall Conference   4-0

285. **Carlisle United (H)**
     March 1990, Division 4   4-3

286. **Exeter City (H)**
     May 1989, Division 4   5-0

287. **Rochdale (A)**
     November 1987, Division 4   5-0

288. **Tranmere Rovers (A)**
     Sepember 1986, Division 4   5-0

289. **Peterborough United (H)**
     April 1986, Division 4   4-0

290. **Southend United (A)**
     January 1985, Division 4   4-0

ALEC CHAMBERLAIN

291. In what year did Alec make his U's debut - 1981, 1982 or 1983?

292. In what position did Alec play?

293. During 1983/1984 Alec played in every League game. What other U's player did so - Keith Bowen, Tony Adcock or Steve Wignall?

294. Which U's manager handed Alex his debut as Mike Walker was injured?

295. For which team did Alec play between 1988 and 1993 - Chelsea, Watford or Luton Town?

296. In what season did Alex win 'player of the year' for Colchester?

297. In 2005 Alec was awarded his testimonial whilst playing for Watford. Against which top-flight team did Watford lose this match 2-1 - Charlton Athletic, West Ham United or Crystal Palace?

298. In what year was Alec born?

299. How many League appearances did Alec make for Colchester United - 88, 188 or 288?

300. When Alec left Layer Road, which top-flight club did he join?

RICHARD WILKINS

301.   In what year did Richard make his Colchester debut -
       1985, 1986 or 1987?

302.   When Richard left Layer Road in 1990, which club did he
       join?

303.   In December 1997 Richard scored two goals, and Aaron
       Skelton got the other, in a 3-2 win against which side -
       Luton Town, Northampton Town or Cambridge United?

304.   Richard joined the U's for his second spell in 1996.
       Which club did he sign from?

305.   Following on from the previous question, which
       manager brought him back to Layer Road for his second
       spell - George Burley, Steve Wignall or Steve Whitton?

306.   In February 1999 Richard scored against which team in
       a 2-1 win?

307.   In July 2002 Richard played against which club in his
       testimonial match with Colchester losing 3-1 - Arsenal,
       West Ham United or Tottenham Hotspur?

308.   After leaving Layer Road, Richard was appointed
       manager of which club?

309.   Against which club did Richard score two goals in a 2-1
       home win in February 1997 - Barnet, Leyton Orient or
       Brentford?

310.   Against which London side did Richard make his 250th
       appearance in April 1999?

TONY ENGLISH

311.   Which Midlands club did Tony join in 1983 - Walsall, Aston Villa or Coventry City?

312.   In what year did Tony make his League debut?

313.   How many League goals did Tony score in his 36 League appearances during 1988/1989 - 4, 8 or 12?

314.   Against which Essex side did Tony make his U's debut?

315.   During September 1994 Tony was awarded his testimonial against Ipswich Town at Layer Road. What was the score - 3-1, 3-2 or 3-3?

316.   In what year was Tony born in Luton?

317.   How many goals did Tony score in his first season at Layer Road - 1, 3 or 5?

318.   During 1993/1994 Tony played in every League game. Which other U's player did the same?

319.   Tony scored a League hat-trick in September 1986, against which team in a 3-0 home win - Leyton Orient, Torquay United or Shrewsbury Town?

320.   In what year did Tony leave Layer Road?

POT LUCK - 2

321.   From what East Anglian club did Colchester sign Adrian Coote in 2001 - Ipswich Town, Ipswich Wanderers or Norwich City?

322.   Which goalkeeper scored the winning goal in a 2-1 away win against Wycombe Wanderers in September 1991?

323.   Which team did Colchester play in the FA Trophy Final in May 1992 - Oxford United, Torquay United or Witton Albion?

324.   Which player scored 7 League goals in 11 games whilst on loan during 1973/1974 to help the U's to promotion to Division 3?

325.   In May 1979 Colchester recorded their highest away win (then a club record) against which club - Blackpool, Tranmere Rovers or Exeter City?

326.   Can you name the U's manager who took over in November 1987 and then left in October 1988?

327.   Which player was Mick Wadsworth's first signing (loan) for the U's in February 1999 - Joe Dunne, Warren Aspinall or Steve Whitton?

328.   Who were the only two players to play in every League match during the 1992/1993 season in Division 3?

329.   Which team did Colchester play in the Auto Windscreen Shield final in April 1997 - Chesterfield, Carlisle United or Blackpool?

330.   Can you name 7 of the starting 11 of Colchester's team against Whitton Albion in the 3-1 winning Vauxhall FA Trophy final in May 1992?

RAY CRAWFORD

331. Against which club did Ray make his U's League debut in August 1970 in a 1-0 home win - Hull City, Hartlepool or Grimsby Town?

332. Against which team did Ray score his first League goal in August 1970 in a 2-0 away win?

333. Which manager signed Ray for the U's - Dick Graham, Bobby Roberts or Cyril Lea?

334. The U's bought Ray for £3,000 from which club?

335. For which team did Ray play between 1958 and 1963 and then again between 1965 and 1969 - Norwich City, Southend United or Ipswich Town?

336. Against which two teams did Ray score hat-tricks during 1970/1971?

337. Ray scored two goals in a giant-killing 3-2 victory against which top-flight side in the FA Cup 5th round in 1971 - Liverpool, Leicester City or Leeds United?

338. Ray won two caps for England during his playing career, scoring how many goals?

339. Which England manager handed Ray his England debut in 1961 and later his second cap in 1962 - Alf Ramsey, Walter Winterbottom or Ron Greenwood?

340. How many goals did Ray score during his U's career in his 45 appearances for the club?

MIKE WALKER

341. Against which team did Mike take over as manager of the U's for the first time as caretaker manager - Rotherham, Blackpool or Rochdale?

342. Following on from the previous question, in which year was this?

343. How much did Colchester pay for Mike Walker when he joined in 1973 - £1,500, £2,500 or £4,000?

344. Following on from the previous question, from which club did the U's sign Mike?

345. In which year was Mike appointed manager of the U's, only to be sacked the year after - 1985, 1986 or 1987?

346. For which country did Mike win under-23 caps during his playing career?

347. What is the name of Mike's son, the former England and Spurs goalkeeper - Derek, Ian or Steven?

348. During the 1990s Mike guided which club to their highest ever position of 3rd in the Premier League, therefore winning a place in Europe for the first time?

349. How many times did Mike win U's' 'player of the year' - 3, 4 or 5?

350. Which manager took over at Layer Road when Mike left Colchester?

THE 1980s

351. Against which top-flight north-east side did the U's play in the 1982 FA Cup?

352. In what position did Colchester finish in the League during 1984/1985 in Division 4 - 1st, 5th or 7th?

353. In 1982 Allan Hunter took over at Layer Road as player/manager, moving from which club?

354. How many hat-tricks did Colchester score during 1985/1986 - 3, 4 or 5?

355. Colchester played Manchester United in the League Cup in November 1983 and lost 2-0. Can you name the two players that scored?

356. Which player won 'player of the year' during 1986/1987 - Mike Walker, Rudi Hedman or Perry Groves?

357. Which player made a scoring debut in a 3-0 win in August 1987 against Burnley after signing from Torquay?

358. Against which team did Colchester play in the 1986/1987 semi-final play-offs, losing 2-0 on aggregate - Wycombe, Wolverhampton Wanderers or Walsall?

359. Can you name the three players who played in every League game during the 1981/1982 season?

360. Which future U's manager won 'player of the year' in 1982/1983 - George Burley, Ian Atkins or Mike Walker?

THE 1990s

361. During the 1991/1992 season Colchester scored how many goals (in all competitions) - 199, 121 or 123?

362. Which goalkeeper made his League debut on the opening day of the season in August 1992 against Lincoln in a 2-1 home win?

363. Which League did Colchester win in 1991/1992 - Division 3, Division 4 or The Vauxhall Conference?

364. How many games did Colchester win in their championship success during 1991/1992 in the Vauxhall Conference?

365. Which 19-year-old Arsenal star did Colchester sign on loan during 1997/1998, making 11 appearances and scoring 4 goals - Guy Branston, Isiah Rankin or Nicky Haydon?

366. Which player scored 26 League goals in 40 appearances during 1991/1992?

367. Who was the only player to score a hat-trick for the U's during 1993/1994 - Steve Whitton, Steve Brown or Mark Kinsella?

368. The Hunt brothers in 1961, the English brothers in 1986 and which brothers in 1998 scored in the same game away to Shrewsbury?

369. During the 1998/1999 season how many players did the U's use - 15, 25 or 35?

370. Which two U's goalkeepers got sent off in the same game in October 1993 in a 5-0 away defeat to Hereford?

JIM SMITH

371. In what year what Jim born - 1938, 1940 or 1942?

372. At which club was Jim's first managerial appointment?

373. Of what Division did Jim guide Colchester to be winners in 1974 - Division 2, Division 3 or Division 4?

374. What did Jim win in his first month in charge at Layer Road?

375. In which year was Jim appointed player/manager at Layer Road - 1970, 1972 or 1974?

376. In Jim's first full season in charge, to which position in the League did he guide the U's?

377. Which manager took over as U's boss when Jim left Layer Road - Cyril Lea, Bobby Roberts or Allan Hunter?

378. What is Jim's nickname in the world of football?

379. Jim was appointed manager of which team in March 2006 - Derby County, Oxford United or Sunderland?

380. When Jim left Layer Road, which team did he join as manager?

POSITIONS IN THE LEAGUE

MATCH THE SEASON WITH THE POSITION THE U'S ACHIEVED

381.	2005/2006	6th
382.	1997/1998	22nd
383.	1991/1992	6th
384.	1986/1987	1st
385.	1982/1983	2nd
386.	1980/1981	3rd
387.	1975/1976	4th
388.	1973/1974	5th
389.	1970/1971	22nd
390.	1968/1969	6th

PLAYER OF THE YEAR

MATCH THE PLAYER WITH THE SEASON IN WHICH HE WON THE AWARD

391.	Richard Wilkins	1982/1983
392.	Steve Whitton	2005/2006
393.	Paul Roberts	1993/1994
394.	Scott Barrett	1997/1998
395.	Colin Hill	1980/1981
396.	Mike Walker	1994/1995
397.	Mike Walker	1992/1993
398.	Mark Kinsella	1998/1999
399.	David Greene	1990/1991
400.	Wayne Brown	1988/1989

IAN ALLINSON

401. Against which team did Ian make his League debut as a substitute in a 2-2 draw in April 1975 - Blackpool, Blackburn Rovers or Preston North End?

402. Which manager gave Ian his U's debut?

403. During 1981/1982 Ian played in 42 League matches for the U's, scoring how many goals - 21, 25 or 29?

404. Ian scored 22 League goals in 1982/1983, making him U's top scorer that season. In how many of the 46 games did he play?

405. Against which club did Ian score his first goals in August 1976 - Rochdale, Rotherham or Preston North End?

406. In which year was Ian born in Stevenage?

407. In December 1988 Ian re-signed for Colchester from which club - Southend United, Luton Town or Norwich City?

408. Ian scored his first goal in his second spell for the club in January 1989, against which club in a 2-2 draw?

409. Ian was the only player to play in every League game during 1982/1983. How many goals did he score - 20, 22 or 24?

410. In 1984 Ian left Layer Road and joined which top-flight club?

POT LUCK - 3

411. How many League goals did Jamie Moralee score for the U's in his 27 League appearances - 0, 1 or 2?

412. Can you name Colchester United's first playing substitute, who played against Rochdale in September 1965?

413. Who was England's first full international to play for Colchester - Jackie Robinson, Ray Crawford or Mike Walker?

414. Which Colchester player achieved the lowest ever number of goals for a top goalscorer during 1975/1976, with 6 goals?

415. In January 1995 which top-flight side did Colchester play in the FA Cup 3rd round - Crystal Palace, Arsenal or Wimbledon?

416. In April 1986 which Colchester United brothers got sent off in the same game, against Crewe Alexandra?

417. Which player got sent off in his League debut in August 1988 against York City in a 1-0 home win - Dave Barnett, Mark Kinsella or Perry Groves?

418. During 1992/1993 which player won under-21 caps for the Republic of Ireland to become the first U's player to win them?

419. In what year was Colchester's first appearance at Wembley - 1988, 1990 or 1992?

420. Against which team was Bobby Roberts' first game in charge in August 1975 in a 2-1 defeat to Bobby Charlton's side?

ROGER OSBORNE

421. From which club did Colchester sign Roger - Arsenal, Ipswich Town or West Ham United?

422. In what year was Roger signed by Bobby Roberts?

423. Roger made his U's debut in a 2-1 win, setting up both goals, against which club - Bournemouth, Burnley or Blackpool?

424. Roger scored the winning goal in the FA Cup final in 1978 for his previous side, against which team at Wembley?

425. How many goals did Roger score for the U's during his career - 9, 11 or 13?

426. In what position did Roger play during his playing career?

427. Which U's manager signed Roger for Colchester United - Jim Smith, Bobby Roberts or Cyril Lea?

428. In what year was Roger born?

429. Roger made 39 League appearances during 1981/1982, scoring how many goals for the U's - 3, 4 or 5?

430. In what year did Roger win 'player of the year' at Layer Road?

BOBBY SVARC

431. Against which team did Bobby make his U's debut in December 1972?

432. Against which club did Bobby score his first U's goal in February 1973 - Barnsley, Blackpool or Carlisle United?

433. Bobby scored after 45 seconds on the opening day of the 1973/1974 season, against which club in the 1-0 away win?

434. How many goals did Bobby score in his first season at Layer Road - 6, 8 or 10?

435. Which U's manager gave Bobby his Colchester debut in 1972?

436. In November 1973 Bobby scored all four goals in a 4-0 away win in Division 4, against which team - Chester City, Chesterfield or Derby County?

437. During 1974/1975 Bobby played in 42 League games, scoring how many goals?

438. How many goals did Bobby score in his 116 League appearances for the U's in his career - 59, 61 or 63?

439. In which year was Bobby born in Leicester?

440. During 1973/1974 Bobby played in all 46 League games in Division 4. Which two other players did the same - Ray Harford and Mike Walker, Ray Harford and Steve Leslie, or Mike Walker and Phil Thomas?

PERRY GROVES

441. Perry made his U's debut during April 1982, against which club in a 2-1 home defeat - Darlington, Bournemouth or Scunthorpe United?

442. Which U's manager handed Perry his U's debut?

443. In what year was Perry born - 1961, 1963 or 1965?

444. Perry scored his first U's League goal in September 1982; against which team in a 4-1 home win?

445. Perry scored two goals, Keith Bowen scored two and Tony Adcock the other in a 5-2 away win in January 1985, against which side - Southend United, Northampton or Luton Town?

446. Can you name the four U's managers that Perry played under at Layer Road?

447. What nationality is Perry - Irish, Welsh or English?

448. Perry left Layer Road in September 1986 to join which club?

449. Following on from the previous question, which manager bought Perry for his new side - David O'Leary, Jim Smith or George Graham?

450. Against which team did Perry score two hat-tricks in the 1985/1986 season, one in the League and one in the League Cup?

PLAY-OFF FINAL
WINNERS - 1998

451. Which club did Colchester beat in the final - Torquay United, Brentford or Hereford?

452. What was the score in the final?

453. Which team did the U's beat in the semi-final, giving Colchester an aggregate score of 3-2 - Brentford, Luton Town or Barnet?

454. Where was the final played?

455. In what position did Colchester finish in Division 3 - 4th, 5th or 6th?

456. Who played in goal for the U's in the play-off final?

457. What was the attendance in the final - 17,486, 18,486 or 19,486?

458. Who was Colchester's top goalscorer with 8 League goals and also appeared in the play-off final for the U's?

459. Who was the only player to appear in every League game during the promotion-winning season - Richard Wilkins, Carl Emberson or Joe Dunne?

460. Which two players made substitute appearances in the final?

CHRIS IWELUMO

461. What nationality is Chris - English, Scottish or Welsh?

462. For which team did Chris play between 1996 and 1998?

463. In what year did Chris sign for the U's - 2004, 2005 or 2006?

464. Chris played in all 46 League games in his first season at Layer Road, scoring how many goals?

465. For which team did Chris make 84 League appearances, scoring 15 goals, between 2000 and 2004 - Sunderland, Stoke City or Southampton?

466. In October 2005 the U's beat which team 3-2 at home, with Chris scoring two goals?

467. Against which team did Chris make his U's League debut?

468. In November 2005 Chris scored two goals against Blackpool in a 3-2 win. Who got the other U's goal?

469. At which German team did Chris spend 6 months on loan before joining the U's - Bayern Munich, Alemania Aachen or Eintracht Frankfurt?

470. Which U's manager signed Chris for Colchester United?

2005/2006 SQUAD NUMBERS

*MATCH THE PLAYER WITH THE SQUAD NUMBER
HE WORE DURING THE SEASON*

471.	Wayne Brown	18
472.	Richard Garcia	1
473.	John White	5
474.	Karl Duguid	26
475.	Kevin Watson	13
476.	Tony Thorpe	28
477.	Aidan Davison	2
478.	Greg Halford	7
479.	Liam Chilvers	17
480.	Dean Gerken	6

KEMAL IZZET

481. Which top-flight team did Kemal sign for in 1998 and left to join the U's in 2001 - Charlton Athletic, Chelsea or Coventry City?

482. Against which club did Kemal make his U's debut in March 2001 in a 3-1 home win?

483. In which year was Kemal born - 1980, 1981 or 1982?

484. In April 2001 Kemal scored his first U's goal against which team in a 2-2 home draw?

485. Which manager bought Kemal for the U's in 2001 - Steve Whitton, Phil Parkinson or Mick Wadsworth?

486. In October 2002 Kemal scored two goals in a 2-0 home win, against which club?

487. How many goals did Kemal score for the U's during 2002/2003, in all competitions - 6, 8 or 10?

488. During the 2005/2006 promotion season which squad number did Kemal wear?

489. How much did Colchester pay for Kemal - free transfer, £10,000 or £50,000?

490. What in the name of Kemal's brother, the famous Turkish international footballer?

POT LUCK - 4

491. When Neil Gregory left in 2000, which Essex club did he join?

492. What nationality was defender David Greene - Welsh, English or Irish?

493. Which Canadian international goalkeeper played 11 games for the U's in 1988 whilst on loan from Ipswich Town?

494. During 2005/2006 which player did Colchester get on loan from Blackpool - Billy Clarke, Scott Vernon or Mark Yeates?

495. Who was player/manager during 1990/1991 for the U's?

496. Can you name who managed the U's between 1955 and 1963 - Benny Fenton, Jim Smith or Ted Fenton?

497. Which Tottenham midfielder spent two months on loan at Layer Road between March and May 2003?

498. In 1981 Roy McDonough made his debut, scoring in a 2-1 home win, against who - Blackpool, Burnley or Tranmere Rovers?

499. Can you name 7 of the starting 11 players who played in the Auto Windscreen Shield final in April 1997?

500. Which East Anglian team tried to sign Mark Kinsella in March 1994, offering £110,000 and a player - Ipswich Town, Ipswich Wanderers or Norwich City?

PLAYER OF THE YEAR WINNERS

RE-ARRANGE THE LETTERS TO REVEAL THE NAME OF A
PLAYER WHO HAS WON THIS AWARD WHILST AT THE U'S

501. SCRIH YFR

502. NRAIB LALH

503. VNIKE MNRREEB

504. YRA WRDORFAC

505. EETVS NLLAGIW

506. KNCIY MTIHS

507. KMEI RALWKE

508. NLOCI LIHL

509. DDAIV REEENG

510. NOHJ GGTTROAF

COLCHESTER/IPSWICH
CONNECTIONS

*RE-ARRANGE THE LETTERS TO REVEAL THE NAME OF A
PLAYER WHO HAS PLAYED FOR BOTH THE U'S AND IPSWICH*

511. VIDDA GGRREYO

512. KICM LLKTOCEWS

513. RRVEOT YPNEUT

514. OYBBB NHUT

515. IHSRC EEELBK

516. TTUIS EBBLMAR

517. LINE OYGGERR

518. GRICA RTSOERF

519. EETVS TNOTIHW

520. NSOAJ ZZLLEOD

HAT-TRICK HEROES

RE-ARRANGE THE LETTERS TO REVEAL THE NAME OF A
PLAYER WHO HAS SCORED A HAT-TRICK FOR THE U'S

521.   NOYT CCOKDA

522.   RRYEP VSOREG

523.   YRO OONcGHUDM

524.   OYBBB UGGOH

525.   NIMOS EOWL

526.   NILCO DWROOGA

527.   EAVD MMNOSIS

528.   YRO YSSEAM

529.   EEVTS NRWOB

530.   NOHJ TGTGAORF

PROMOTION SQUAD - 1997/1998

RE-ARRANGE THE LETTERS TO REVEAL THE NAME OF A PLAYER WHO WAS PART OF THE PROMOTION SQUAD

531. RNOAA LNEKOTS

532. RRDIACH NWIIKSL

533. LAUP HSAAARBM

534. ADDVI YGORREG

535. LCRA NMOESERB

536. NOYT KOLC

537. KMRA EASL

538. RPTEE EYRALWC

539. EEVTS BSREOF

540. DDVIA EEENRG

SCORERS FOR THE U'S

RE-ARRANGE THE LETTERS TO REVEAL THE NAME OF
A PLAYER WHO HAS SCORED FOR THE U'S

541. LARK GDDUUI

542. LPUA KELCUB

543. TCOTS EHMLIScG

544. YNOT SNNIED

545. NAERRD WRBOOX

546. LPUA STERORB

547. NOJH RRENAW

548. EAVD SHNSWTRLUIDE

549. YBBBO EOGDH

550. AYR DCOAWRRF

FA CUP PLAYERS - 1971

*RE-ARRANGE THE LETTERS TO REVEAL THE NAME OF
A PLAYER WHO HAS PLAYED FOR THE CLUB*

551. HAAMRG MHTIS

552. YRA DARWRCOF

553. EAVD NSOIMMS

554. KCIM HNOAM

555. NIARB SWIEL

556. NOJH ALRIUK

557. NIARB BSBIG

558. ONHJ RILHGSTIC

559. NRAIB VYERGA

560. NKE NSEOJ

PLAYERS OF THE 1980s

RE-ARRANGE THE LETTERS TO REVEAL THE NAME OF
A PLAYER WHO HAS PLAYED FOR CLUB

561. YMCIK KOOC

562. VEETS LLNGIWA

563. LHIP NMAEOLC

564. EVTES LLEESI

565. TRTEAWS NHOOTSU

566. EYRPR SGVEOR

567. CELA BNIAELRMACH

568. YONT CCKODA

569. IRUD NDAMEH

570. YNKCI TTRENOTACH

CONFERENCE PROMOTION SQUAD - 1991/1992

RE-ARRANGE THE LETTERS TO REVEAL THE NAME OF A PLAYER WHO HAS PLAYED FOR THE CLUB

571. KICYN TMIHS

572. LAPU RRSEBOT

573. KARM LLINKAES

574. NARERW DDALON

575. TTOCS TRTREAB

576. ETEVS MGcINVA

577. NHUAS OTTILEL

578. YONT LSHIGNE

579. SNOAJ KOCO

580. YRGA ENTENTB

PLAYERS OF THE 1990s

RE-ARRANGE THE LETTERS TO REVEAL THE NAME OF
A PLAYER WHO HAS PLAYED FOR THE CLUB

581. CEIR GSSREUB

582. NOHJ NLAcGHIULM

583. TEESV YOELF

584. LHIP SOAHMT

585. HONJ OATTRGFG

586. JNOH MWSAIILL

587. VTEES LLSEEY

588. NOILC ODORAWG

589. LAUP RYED

590. SEEVT HWITGR

2006/2007 SQUAD

RE-ARRANGE THE LETTERS TO REVEAL THE NAME OF
A PLAYER WHO WAS IN THE SQUAD

591. NEHNIJO KNOACSJ

592. DIHRRAC AARICG

593. GGER DALROFH

594. ORNAIM HETIK

595. NVIEK SWTNOA

596. TPA DNWALIB

597. EAIMJ YGU

598. LSLSEUR DONP

599. SHRIC LOWIUME

600. LARK GDIDUU

U'S GOALKEEPERS

*RE-ARRANGE THE LETTERS TO REVEAL THE NAME OF
A PLAYER WHO HAS PLAYED FOR THE CLUB*

601. NAADI SNDIVAO

602. NOHJ AECRG

603. KARM NALOWT

604. LARC NBRSOEME

605. NOHJ EEELKY

606. HOJN GTEEEHSIRHWC

607. CEAL LBMCNAAHIRE

608. OJNH NYcMLLAI

609. MGHAAR HSTMI

610. EMKI RWELAK

PROMOTION SQUAD - 2005/2006

RE-ARRANGE THE LETTERS TO REVEAL THE NAME OF A PLAYER WHO WAS PART OF THE PROMOTION SQUAD

611. NIAAD VNOISAD

612. TPA NBDWILA

613. NAED NGKEER

614. LRAK GDDUUI

615. NOHJ EWTIH

616. NIEVK TWNOSA

617. ERGG LHFAODR

618. LEAMK TZEZI

619. EEGROG KEOIBOL

620. SHICR OWMIUEL

LEAGUE OPPONENTS
- 2006/2007

*RE-ARRANGE THE LETTERS TO REVEAL THE NAME OF
A TEAM THAT THE U'S PLAYED DURING 2006/2007*

621. YBNAERLS

622. RLTECEISE YICT

623. HSPCIIW WONT

624. OULTN ONWT

625. OESKT IYTC

626. INWOHCR YCIT

627. NELYRUB

628. SEDEL TUENDI

629. MMIIANHRGB TICY

630. NRTEOSP HOTRN DEN

U'S STRIKERS

*RE-ARRANGE THE LETTERS TO REVEAL THE NAME OF
A PLAYER WHO HAS PLAYED FOR THE CLUB*

631.   OYNT KACCOD

632.   YBLADER NAELL

633.   SRIHC LOWIEMU

634.   EMIAJ EURNOTC

635.   NOYT PTEOHR

636.   TCOTS HIcGMELS

637.   AOLNAM RRTOSE AUL LAU

638.   VETES TWINOTH

639.   YAR DRWOFARC

640.   NOHJ GTGTAORF

LEADING SCORERS

RE-ARRANGE THE LETTERS TO REVEAL THE NAME OF
A PLAYER WHO WAS A LEADING SCORER DURING A SEASON

641. IAVDD RRGGOYE

642. ROIAM HWSLA

643. NEIVK MBEERRN

644. YRO UHONcDOGM

645. YANDN TIHGL

646. LNIE YRGOREG

647. EALD PTTSEME

648. NRAIB IEWLS

649. YTON CCKODA

650. SHIRC RYF

PLAYERS - 1992/1993

651. RGAY TBNTENE

652. LARC BNREOMSE

653. LPAU WEELLN

654. ALUP ESBRTRO

655. KARM SKALLENI

656. OIMNS TETSB

657. BRTEOR RUXVEEED

658. EETRP WCYRAEL

659. RBTEOR SKNPIOH

660. EDRF RREABB

PLAYERS - 1982/1983

*RE-ARRANGE THE LETTERS TO REVEAL THE NAME OF
A PLAYER WHO HAS PLAYED FOR THE CLUB*

661. NAI NNOSILLA

662. ETEVS GLLAINW

663. RRGEO NOOREBS

664. SNNIED HNOOGRUL

665. FJEF LULH

666. KCIYM KOCO

667. LPIH NCALMEO

668. CIKM KRCEAP

669. EANYW RWAD

670. NLALA THNERU

U'S DEFENDERS

*RE-ARRANGE THE LETTERS TO REVEAL THE NAME OF
A PLAYER WHO HAS PLAYED FOR THE CLUB*

671. VAIDD EEENRG

672. NLAA TWIHE

673. TPA NAWLIDB

674. KICYM OKOC

675. REETP WCYELAR

676. EJO NENUD

677. NMITRA GGRRENIA

678. LHIP NCMAELO

679. NMOIS TSTEB

680. YNTO TYcRHACM

PLAYERS OF THE 1990s

*RE-ARRANGE THE LETTERS TO REVEAL THE NAME OF
A PLAYER WHO HAS PLAYED FOR THE CLUB*

681. YONT LHSEGNI

682. TSCOT RTRTEBA

683. KARM NKSIEALL

684. EEVTS VNIcMGA

685. RNITAM NGIGRRAE

686. NLAA KSCNEID

687. EETRP WYELARC

688. NOHJ EEETGHWIRSHC

689. AIVDD YROGEGR   .

690. RAKM LAES

MANAGERS OF THE U'S

RE-ARRANGE THE LETTERS TO REVEAL THE NAME
OF PAST COLCHESTER UNITED MANAGER

691. LRYIC AEL

692. LHIP KNOPNSIRA

693. ETEVS LNLAGWI

694. EEOGRG RBUYEL

695. NRAMON RHTENU

696. KICD AMAHRG

697. CIMK LILSM

698. ETVES TNOTIWH

699. OYR NOHGUcODM

700. NAI KSNTIA

ANSWERS

2005/2006 - UP TO THE CHAMPIONSHIP

1. Phil Parkinson
2. Gillingham
3. Yeovil Town
4. Mark Yeates
5. Pat Baldwin
6. Chelsea
7. Barnsley (won 1-0)
8. 7
9. 22
10. 17

CLUB HISTORY & STADIUM

11. 1937
12. Derby County
13. Reading
14. Geraint Williams
15. 1950/1951
16. Neil Gregory in 1998 and Adrian Coote in 2001
17. Leyton Orient
18. Micky Cook
19. Watney Cup
20. Bobby Hunt

NATIONALTIES

21. Karl Duguid — English
22. Gareth Williams — Welsh
23. Mark Kinsella — Irish
24. George Elokobi — Cameroon
25. Chris Iwelumo — Scottish
26. Mark Yeates — Irish
27. Richard Garcia — Australian
28. Lomana Tresor Lua-Lua — Democratic Republic of Congo
29. Pat Baldwin — English
30. Marino Keith — Scottish

POT LUCK - 1

31. Ipswich Town

32.	Chelmsford
33.	Queens Park Rangers
34.	Aidan Davison
35.	8
36.	Bobby Robson
37.	1998
38.	6
39.	Southampton
40.	Blackburn Rovers

WHERE DID THEY GO?

41.	Simon Brown	Hibernian
42.	Mick Stockwell	Heybridge Swifts
43.	Rowan Vine	Portsmouth
44.	Paul Abrahams	Kettering Town
45.	Scott McGleish	Northampton Town
46.	Jamie Cade	Crawley Town
47.	Mark Kinsella	Charlton Athletic
48.	Roy McDonough	Southend United
49.	Bobby Bowry	Gravesend & Northfleet
50.	Gavin Johnson	Boston United

STEVE WHITTON

51.	1960
52.	£10,000
53.	Ipswich Town
54.	Doncaster Rovers
55.	Walsall
56.	1994
57.	1999 (August)
58.	Scarborough
59.	Phil Parkinson
60.	West Ham United

NAME THE YEAR

| 61. | Tony Adcock signed from Luton Town on a free transfer | 1995 |

73

62.	Colchester beat Leamington 9-1 in the FA Cup (1st round)	2005
63.	Leyton Orient beat Colchester 8-0 in Division 4	1989
64.	Carl Emberson signed from Millwall costing £25,000	1994
65.	Colchester finished 2nd in League One behind Southend United	2006
66.	Colchester beat Leeds United 3-2 in the FA Cup 5th round	1971
67.	Mark Kinsella left Colchester to join Charlton Athletic	1996
68.	Colchester beat Bradford City 9-1 in Division 4	1961
69.	Colchester lost 3-1 to Chelsea in the 5th round of the FA Cup	2006
70.	Steve McGavin played his first game for the U's	1992

LOMANA TRESOR LUA-LUA

71. Mick Wadsworth
72. Chesterfield
73. Newcastle United
74. Portsmouth
75. 1980
76. Democratic Republic of Congo
77. Queens Park Rangers
78. Jamie Moralee
79. Queens Park Rangers (League Cup hat-trick, August 2000)
80. Karl Duguid and Steve McGavin

PHIL PARKINSON

81. 2003
82. Bury
83. 1967
84. Southampton
85. England XI

86.   Parky
87.   1998 and 1999 (1997/1998 and 1998/1999 seasons)
88.   Midfield (central)
89.   Reading
90.   24

COLCHESTER MANAGERS

91.	Steve Whitton	1999 to 2003
92.	Mike Walker	1986 to 1987
93.	Roy McDonough	1991 to 1994
94.	Allan Hunter	1982 to 1983
95.	George Burley	1994
96.	Jim Smith	1972 to 1975
97.	Ted Fenton	1946 to 1948
98.	Steve Wignall	1995 to 1999
99.	Dick Graham	1968 to 1972
100.	Mick Mills	1990

JASON DOZZELL

101.   1998
102.   Midfield
103.   Ipswich Town
104.   4
105.   Manchester City
106.   9
107.   Steve Wignall
108.   Cambridge United
109.   Chesterfield
110.   Tottenham Hotspur

KARL DUGUID

111.   Hereford United
112.   Torquay United, won 3-2 (January 1996)
113.   Steve Wignall
114.   Tony Adcock and David Gregory
115.   35 (26 starts and 9 substitute appearances)
116.   Torn knee ligament
117.   Milton Keynes Dons

118. Doogie
119. Oldham Athletic
120. 7

HAT-TRICK HEROES - 1

121.	v. Queens Park Rangers (A) August 2000, Won 4-1	L. T. Lua-Lua
122.	v. Torquay United (H) September 1995, Won 5-2	Tony Adcock
123.	v. Bury (H) September 1993, Won 4-1	Steve Brown
124.	v. Barrow (H) May 1992, Won 5-0	Mike Masters
125.	v. Slough Town (A) August 1991, Won 4-2	Roy McDonough
126.	v. Bath City (H) August 1991, Won 5-0	Gary Bennett
127.	v. Stockport County (H) March 1987, Won 5-1	Simon Lowe
128.	v. Torquay United (H) September 1986, Won 3-0	Tony English
129.	v. Peterborough United (H) April 1986, Won 5-0	Tony English
130.	v. Preston North End (H) April 1986, Won 4-0	Tom English

GEORGE BURLEY

131. 1994
132. Roy McDonough
133. Torquay United
134. 38 years old
135. Motherwell
136. Dale Roberts
137. 7 (5 starts and 2 substitute appearances)
138. Ipswich Town
139. Scarborough
140. Southampton

BOBBY HUNT

141. 1942
142. 81
143. Centre forward
144. Bobby Fenton
145. 37
146. Millwall
147. Bradford City
148. Doncaster Rovers
149. Charlton Athletic
150. Northampton Town

MARK KINSELLA

151. Irish
152. 48
153. 1989/1990
154. Halifax
155. Aston Villa
156. Jock Wallace
157. Czech Republic
158. 6
159. Torquay United
160. Charlton Athletic

1971 FA CUP RUN

161. Leeds United
162. Crawford (2) and Simmons
163. Everton (5-0)
164. 5-0
165. Dick Graham
166. Graham Smith
167. Ringmer
168. Reaching the FA quarter-final was a record for a Division 4 club
169. 16,000
170. Cambridge United

MICK STOCKWELL

171. Chelmsford

172. Ipswich Town
173. Steve Whitton
174. Free Transfer
175. Swindon Town
176. Bournemouth
177. Ross Johnson
178. Queens Park Rangers
179. 11
180. Heybridge Swifts

BIG COLCHESTER WINS - 1

181.	v. Chesterfield (A)	
	August 2001, Division 2	Won 6-3
182.	v. Bristol Rovers (H)	
	January 2000, Division 2	Won 5-4
183.	v. Macclesfield Town (H)	
	March 1998, Division 3	Won 5-1
184.	v. Lincoln City (H)	
	November 1996, Division 3	Won 7-1
185.	v. Torquay United (H)	
	September 1995, Associate Members Cup	Won 5-2
186.	v. Yeading (H)	
	November 1994, FA Cup	Won 7-1
187.	v. Fulham (H)	
	April 1995, Division 3	Won 5-2
188.	v. Wycombe Wanderers (A)	
	September 1993, Division 3	Won 5-2
189.	v. Bath City (H)	
	August 1991, Vauxhall Conference	Won 5-0
190.	v. Yeovil Town (H)	
	September 1991, Vauxhall Conference	Won 4-0

DAVID GREGORY

191. Peterborough United
192. Barnet
193. Torquay United
194. Ipswich Town
195. Canvey Island

196. *Wigan Athletic (October 1996)*
197. *19*
198. *Colchester*
199. *Barnet*
200. *Steve Wignall*

WHERE DID THEY COME FROM?

201.	*Thomas Pinault*	*Cannes*
202.	*Gavin Johnson*	*Dunfermline*
203.	*Chris Fry*	*Hereford*
204.	*Sam Stockley*	*Oxford United*
205.	*Pat Baldwin*	*Chelsea*
206.	*Mark Warren*	*Notts County*
207.	*Andy Myers*	*Bradford City*
208.	*Jamie Cade*	*Middlesbrough*
209.	*Liam Chilvers*	*Arsenal*
210.	*Marino Keith*	*Plymouth Argyle*

TONY ADCOCK

211. *London*
212. *Centre forward*
213. *Luton Town*
214. *Carlisle*
215. *Bobby Roberts*
216. *Torquay*
217. *Crewe Alexandra*
218. *Torquay*
219. *31*
220. *Southend United (August 1984) and Chesterfield (February 1985)*

STEVE McGAVIN

221. *1969*
222. *Northampton Town*
223. *Southend United*
224. *Gateshead*
225. *Ian Atkins*
226. *Bath City*
227. *Steve Brown*

228. Steve Whitton
229. Forward
230. Birmingham City

NAME THE YEAR - 2

231.	Simon Clark signed from Leyton Orient on a free transfer	2000
232.	Mick Wadsworth arrived and left as manager	1999
233.	Colchester record their record attendance in the FA Cup against Reading	1948
234.	Peter Crawley signs for the U's from Barnet on a free transfer	1992
235.	Jim Smith takes the job at Layer Road as player/manager	1972
236.	Alec Chamberlain signs for the U's from Ipswich Town	1982
237.	Mike Walker is appointed U's manager	1986
238.	Tony Adcock left and signed for Manchester City for £75,000	1987
239.	Richard Wilkins signs for Colchester from Haverhill Rovers	1986
240.	Steve Wignall leaves as Colchester manager	1999

MICKY COOK

241. Wrexham
242. Crewe Alexandra
243. Dick Graham
244. Full back (defence)
245. Ipswich Town
246. Cyril Lea
247. 1971/1972
248. Swindon Town
249. Mike Walker
250. 613

HAT-TRICK HEROES - 2

251.	v. Southend United (H)	
	January 1986, Won 4-1	Perry Groves
252.	v. Southend United (A)	
	October 1985, Won 4-2	Perry Groves
253.	v. Cambridge United (H)	
	September 1985, Won 4-1	Tony Adcock
254.	v. Chesterfield (H)	
	February 1985, Won 3-1	Tony Adcock
255.	v. Southend United (H)	
	August 1984, Drew 3-3	Tony Adcock
256.	v. Wealdstone (H)	
	December 1983, Won 4-0	Keith Bowen
257.	v. Crewe Alexandra (H)	
	January 1983, Won 4-3	Tony Adcock
258.	Mansfield Town (A)	
	November 1981, Won 3-1	Ian Allinson
259.	Oxford United (H)	
	November 1978, Won 4-2	Bobby Gough
260.	Bournemouth (Vicarage Road)	
	December 1977, Won 4-1	Colin Garwood

WAYNE BROWN

261. Watford
262. Tranmere Rovers
263. Shrewsbury Town (October 1997 in a 1-1 draw)
264. Wrexham
265. Colchester United
266. Leamington
267. Greg Halford and Jamie Cureton
268. Ipswich Town
269. 2005/2006
270. Phil Parkinson

JOE DUNNE

271. Irish
272. Gillingham
273. 6

274. Hartlepool United
275. Chesterfield
276. 1-0 to Colchester United
277. Mansfield Town
278. Dover
279. Steve Whitton
280. Lincoln

BIG COLCHESTER WINS - 2

281. Kettering Town (H)
      October 1991, Bob Lord Trophy   4-0
282. Burton Albion (H)
      November 1991, FA Cup   5-0
283. Barrow (H)
      May 1992, Vauxhall Conference   5-0
284. Northwich Victoria (H)
      September 1990, Vauxhall Conference   4-0
285. Carlisle United (H)
      March 1990, Division 4   4-0
286. Exeter City (H)
      May 1989, Division 4   4-0
287. Rochdale (A)
      November 1987, Division 4   4-1
288. Tranmere Rovers (A)
      September 1986, Division 4   4-3
289. Peterborough United (H)
      April 1986, Division 4   5-0
290. Southend United (A)
      January 1985, Division 4   5-2

ALEC CHAMBERLAIN

291. 1983
292. Goalkeeper
293. Keith Bowen
294. Allan Hunter
295. Luton Town
296. 1984/1985
297. Charlton Athletic

298. 1964
299. 188
300. Everton

RICHARD WILKINS
301. 1986
302. Cambridge United
303. Cambridge United
304. Hereford United
305. Steve Wignall
306. Wigan Athletic
307. Tottenham Hotspur
308. Bury Town
309. Leyton Orient
310. Millwall

TONY ENGLISH
311. Coventry City
312. 1984
313. 8
314. Southend United
315. 3-3
316. 1966
317. 3
318. Mark Kinsella
319. Torquay United
320. 1996

POT LUCK - 2
321. Norwich City
322. Scott Barrett
323. Witton Albion
324. Gary Moore
325. Tranmere Rovers
326. Roger Brown
327. Warren Aspinall
328. Paul Roberts and Nicky Smith
329. Carlisle United

330. Scott Barrett, Warren Donald, Paul Roberts, Mark Kinsella, Tony English, Dave Martin, Jason Cook, Mike Masters, Roy McDonough, Steve McGavin and Nicky Smith

RAY CRAWFORD

331. Hartlepool
332. Barrow
333. Dick Graham
334. Kettering
335. Ipswich Town
336. Crewe Alexandra (September 1970 in Division 4) and Ringmer (November 1970 in the FA Cup)
337. Leeds United
338. 1 (against Austria in 1962)
339. Walter Winterbottom
340. 24

MIKE WALKER

341. Rochdale
342. 1986 (April)
343. £4,000
344. Watford
345. 1986
346. Wales
347. Ian Walker
348. Norwich City
349. 3: 1979/1980, 1980/1981 and 1982/1983
350. Roger Brown

THE 1980s

351. Newcastle United
352. 7th
353. Ipswich Town
354. 5
355. Gordon McQueen and Remi Moses
356. Rudi Hedman
357. Mario Walsh
358. Wolverhampton Wanderers

359. Kevin Bremner, Micky Cook and Mike Walker
360. Mike Walker

THE 1990s
361. 123
362. Paul Newell
363. The Vauxhall Conference
364. 28
365. Isiah Rankin
366. Roy McDonough
367. Steve Brown
368. The Gregory brothers (David and Neil)
369. 35
370. John Keeley and Nathan Munson

JIM SMITH
371. 1940
372. Boston United
373. Division 4
374. Manager of the Month award
375. 1972
376. 3rd
377. Bobby Roberts
378. The Bald Eagle
379. Oxford United
380. Blackburn Rovers

POSITIONS IN THE LEAGUE
381.	2005/2006	2nd
382.	1997/1998	4th
383.	1991/1992	1st
384.	1986/1987	5th
385.	1982/1983	6th
386.	1980/1981	22nd
387.	1975/1976	22nd
388	1973/1974	3rd
389.	1970/1971	6th
390.	1968/1969	6th

PLAYER OF THE YEAR

391.	Richard Wilkins	1997/1998
392.	Steve Whitton	1994/1995
393.	Paul Roberts	1992/1993
394.	Scott Barrett	1990/1991
395.	Colin Hill	1988/1989
396.	Mike Walker	1982/1983
397.	Mike Walker	1980/1981
398.	Mark Kinsella	1993/1994
399.	David Greene	1998/1999
400.	Wayne Brown	2005/2006

IAN ALLINSON

401. Preston North End
402. Jim Smith
403. 21
404. 46 (all of them)
405. Rochdale
406. 1957
407. Luton Town
408. Grimsby Town
409. 22
410. Arsenal

POT LUCK - 3

411. 1
412. Ray Price
413. Ray Crawford
414. Steve Leslie
415. Wimbledon
416. English (Tom and Tony)
417. Dave Barnett
418. Mark Kinsella
419. 1992 (May), against Whitton Albion in the Vauxhall FA Trophy final
420. Preston North End

ROGER OSBORNE

421. Ipswich Town
422. 1981
423. Burnley
424. Arsenal
425. 11
426. Midfield
427. Bobby Roberts
428. 1958
429. 5
430. 1985/1986

BOBBY SVARC

431. Hartlepool
432. Barnsley (home), lost 2-1
433. Barnsley
434. 8
435. Jim Smith
436. Chester City
437. 24
438. 59
439. 1946
440. Ray Harford and Mike Walker

PERRY GROVES

441. Bournemouth
442. Bobby Roberts
443. 1965
444. Blackpool
445. Southend United
446. Bobby Roberts, Allan Hunter, Cyril Lea and Mike Walker
447. English
448. Arsenal
449. George Graham
450. Southend United

PLAY-OFF FINAL WINNERS - 1998

451. Torquay United

452. 1-0 to Colchester
453. Barnet
454. Wembley Stadium
455. 4th
456. Carl Emberson
457. 19,486
458. Neil Gregory
459. Carl Emberson
460. Karl Duguid and Tony Lock

CHRIS IWELUMO

461. Scottish
462. St Mirren
463. 2005
464. 17
465. Stoke City
466. Yeovil Town
467. Gillingham (away), August 2005, lost 2-1
468. Greg Halford
469. Alemania Aachen
470. Phil Parkinson

2005/2006 SQUAD NUMBERS

471.	Wayne Brown	5
472.	Richard Garcia	28
473.	John White	17
474.	Karl Duguid	7
475.	Kevin Watson	6
476.	Tony Thorpe	26
477.	Aidan Davison	1
478.	Greg Halford	2
479.	Liam Chilvers	18
480.	Dean Gerken	13

KEMAL IZZET

481. Charlton Athletic
482. Luton Town
483. 1980

484. Peterborough United
485. Steve Whitton
486. Chesterfield
487. 8
488. 10
489. Free transfer
490. Muzzy Izzet

POT LUCK - 4

491. Canvey Island
492. Irish
493. Craig Forrest
494. Scott Vernon
495. Ian Atkins
496. Benny Fenton
497. Johnnie Jackson
498. Burnley
499. Carl Emberson, Joe Dunne, Paul Gibbs, David Gregory, David Greene, Peter Crawley, Richard Wilkins, Mark Sale, Steve Whitton, Tony Adcock and Paul Abrahams
500. Norwich City

PLAYER OF THE YEAR WINNERS

501. Chris Fry
502. Brian Hall
503. Kevin Bremner
504. Ray Crawford
505. Steve Wignall
506. Nicky Smith
507. Mike Walker
508. Colin Hill
509. David Greene
510. John Froggatt

COLCHESTER/IPSWICH CONNECTIONS

511. David Gregory
512. Mick Stockwell
513. Trevor Putney

514. Bobby Hunt
515. Chris Keeble
516. Titus Bramble
517. Neil Gregory
518. Craig Forrest
519. Steve Whitton
520. Jason Dozzell

HAT-TRICK HEROES
521. Tony Adcock
522. Perry Groves
523. Roy McDonough
524. Bobby Gough
525. Simon Lowe
526. Colin Garwood
527. Dave Simmons
528. Roy Massey
529. Steve Brown
530. John Froggatt

PROMOTION SQUAD - 1997/1998
531. Aaron Skelton
532. Richard Wilkins
533. Paul Abrahams
534. David Gregory
535. Carl Emberson
536. Tony Lock
537. Mark Sale
538. Peter Crawley
539. Steve Forbes
540. David Greene

SCORERS FOR THE U'S
541. Karl Duguid
542. Paul Buckle
543. Scott McGleish
544. Tony Dennis
545. Darren Oxbrow

546. Paul Roberts
547. John Warner
548. Dave Swindlehurst
549. Bobby Hodge
550. Ray Crawford

FA CUP PLAYERS - 1971

551. Graham Smith
552. Ray Crawford
553. Dave Simmons
554. Mick Mahon
555. Brian Lewis
556. John Kurila
557. Brian Gibbs
558. John Gilchrist
559. Brian Garvey
560. Ken Jones

PLAYERS OF THE 1980s

561. Micky Cook
562. Steve Wignall
563. Phil Coleman
564. Steve Leslie
565. Stewart Houston
566. Perry Groves
567. Alec Chamberlain
568. Tony Adcock
569. Rudi Hedman
570. Nicky Chatterton

CONFERENCE PROMOTION SQUAD - 1991/1992

571. Nicky Smith
572. Paul Roberts
573. Mark Kinsella
574. Warren Donald
575. Scott Barrett
576. Steve McGavin
577. Shaun Elliott

578. Tony English
579. Jason Cook
580. Gary Bennett

PLAYERS OF THE 1990s
581. Eric Burgess
582. John McLaughlin
583. Steve Foley
584. Phil Thomas
585. John Froggatt
586. John Williams
587. Steve Lesley
588. Colin Garwood
589. Paul Dyer
590. Steve Wright

2006/2007 SQUAD
591. Johnnie Jackson
592. Richard Garcia
593. Greg Halford
594. Marino Keith
595. Kevin Watson
596. Pat Baldwin
597. Jamie Guy
598. Russell Pond
599. Chris Iwelumo
600. Karl Duguid

U'S GOALKEEPERS
601. Aidan Davison
602. John Grace
603. Mark Walton
604. Carl Emberson
605. John Keeley
606. John Cheesewright
607. Alec Chamberlain
608. John McInally
609. Graham Smith

610.   Mike Walker

PROMOTION SQUAD - 2005/2006

611.   Aidan Davison
612.   Pat Baldwin
613.   Dean Gerken
614.   Karl Duguid
615.   John White
616.   Kevin Watson
617.   Greg Halford
618.   Kemal Izzet
619.   George Elokobi
620.   Chris Iwelumo

LEAGUE OPPONENTS - 2006/2007

621.   Barnsley
622.   Leicester City
623.   Ipswch Town
624.   Luton Town
625.   Stoke City
626.   Norwich City
627.   Burnley
628.   Leeds United
629.   Birmingham City
630.   Preston North End

U'S STRIKERS

631.   Tony Adcock
632.   Bradley Allen
633.   Chris Iwelumo
634.   Jamie Cureton
635.   Tony Thorpe
636.   Scott McGleish
637.   Lomana Tresor Lua Lua
638.   Steve Whitton
639.   Ray Crawford
640.   John Froggatt

LEADING SCORERS

641. David Gregory
642. Mario Walsh
643. Kevin Bremner
644. Roy McDonough
645. Danny Light
646. Neil Gregory
647. Dale Tempest
648. Brian Lewis
649. Tony Adcock
650. Chris Fry

PLAYERS - 1992/1993

651. Gary Bennett
652. Carl Emberson
653. Paul Newell
654. Paul Roberts
655. Mark Kinsella
656. Simon Betts
657. Robert Devereux
658. Peter Crawley
659. Robert Hopkins
660. Fred Barber

PLAYERS - 1982/1983

661. Ian Allinson
662. Steve Wignall
663. Roger Osborne
664. Dennis Loughorn
665. Jeff Hull
666. Micky Cook
667. Phil Coleman
668. Mick Packer
669. Wayne Ward
670. Allan Hunter

U'S DEFENDERS

671. David Greene

672. Alan White
673. Pat Baldwin
674. Micky Cook
675. Peter Crawley
676. Joe Dunne
677. Martin Grainger
678. Phil Coleman
679. Simon Betts
680. Tony McCarthy

PLAYERS OF THE 1990s

681. Tony English
682. Scott Barrett
683. Mark Kinsella
684. Steve McGavin
685. Martin Grainger
686. Alan Dickens
687. Peter Crawley
688. John Cheesewright
689. David Gregory
690. Mark Sale

MANAGERS OF THE U'S

691. Cyril Lea
692. Phil Parkinson
693. Steve Wignall
694. George Burley
695. Norman Hunter
696. Dick Graham
697. Mick Mills
698. Steve Whitton
699. Roy McDonough
700. Ian Atkins

Colchester United
Community Sports Trust

The "Football in the Community" project at Colchester United was established in 1993 before becoming known as the Colchester United Community Sports Trust after a bid to become a company limited by guarantee and a registered charity was successful in 2001. As the Trust evolved towards charitable status a set of aims and objectives were established targeting the promotion of opportunities for those people who may be excluded from mainstream sport (particularly football). This statement of intent offered a vision of working in partnership with communities, and improving the quality of life for individuals and neighbourhoods.

As the Trust expanded it's football provision across north and central Essex it has focussed on enhancing the life chances of both individuals and neighbourhoods. The Trust works closely with partners to offer an inclusive and diverse range of sporting and social opportunities, which has benefited over thirty thousand young people. The Trust currently employs 16 full time staff, 25 part-time staff and twelve volunteers as a company limited by guarantee.

By adapting our ongoing vision, aims and objectives, setting clear targets and implementing sustainable beneficial projects backed by local communities, strong partnerships with local government agencies and business partners were established and the Trust consistently promotes, supports and delivers the Government's agenda on health, education and the sporting well-being of young people.

Website: www.cucst.org.uk

Contact:
Email: info@cucst.org.uk
Telephone : 01206 572378

REVIEWS...

*"This is a book that will keep Colchester United
fans amused for hours!*
- www.culfc.com

"Even U's know-alls will learn a thing or two!"
- Mel Henderson, East Anglian Daily Times and Evening Star

*"WHAT great timing. A top quality quiz book which will answer
many questions about championship club Colchester United that
U's fans will love and quench the curiosity of those supporters not
so familiar with, arguably, Essex's finest. The format is wonderfully
simple and effective that will provide hours of fun and will also act
as a valuable source of information. Terrific value and with £1 going
to Colchester United's Sports Trust, a must for all football fans
and not just those of the Mighty U's."*
- Derek Davis, East Anglian Daily Times

*"Colchester United are the team of the moment,
but how much do you know about them?
You now have an ideal chance to find out. Don't miss out!"*
- Elvin King, Evening Star

REVIEWS...

"This book has so much information in that teaches you a lot about the history of Colchester United - have fun with this!"
- Kem Izzet

"A book which is very educational for any U's fans - enjoy the challenge! I will be testing all the lads on the coach on away trips."
- Pat Baldwin

"Full of facts, figures and history of a great club... Colchester United! I thoroughly enjoyed it all!"
- Greg Halford

"I really enjoyed The Official Colchester United Quiz Book. It will test the memory of every U's fan."
- Roger Osborne

"This quiz book will occupy the minds of anyone on a long trip and will thoroughly test U's fans, both young and old, on their knowledge of the past happenings at the club."
- Phil Parkinson

"The Official Colchester United Quiz Book is a must for all U's supporters, whether they be those who can look back with memories over the contrasting years of fantastic highs and awful lows, or whether they be those new to the ranks, in particular youngsters just setting out on a life-time of supporting the friendliest football club in Britain. This book provides a wealth of material which will appeal to every true U's fan."
- Bob Russell, Member of Parliament (Colchester)